FROM SEA TO SHINING SEA
WRITTEN BY TOMMY WATKINS
AF489290

Henry was new to Lowell.

Lowell was a small town in rural America.

Henry was an immigrant from Scotland.

Being an immigrant, Henry wanted to engage in all the Independence Day activities that Lowell was offering.

6
4

Henry attended the parade first.

The floats drive through the parade, throwing candy to all the kids.

Clowns in little cars drove in progression next.

Henry dropped his phone on the street, and one of the clowns ran over it!

This caused all the clown cars to crash into each other. The parade halted, and everyone attending the parade was upset.

Henry was embarrassed and decided t

head home.

He still wanted to see the fireworks but didn't want everyone in the town to laugh at him because of what happened at the parade.

Henry decided to go to watch the fireworks. Once he arrived, the city official told the townspeople they couldn't watch the fireworks because they hadn't worked with this much dynamite before.

POLIC

Back in Scotland, Henry worked with dynamite all the time.

Henry stepped up to the city official an offered his services for the fireworks show. Henry lit the fireworks and impressed the townspeople.

The townspeople accepted Henry in thei
small town, and Henry felt welcomed i
his new home.

The End

www.ingramcontent.com/pod-product-compliance
Lightning Source LLC
Chambersburg PA
CBHW042118110726
48006CB00002B/679